W9-AXU-701

PIANO • VOCAL • GUITAR
2ND EDITION

FORTY SONGS *for a better* WORLD

ISBN 0-7935-5696-1

HAL•LEONARD®
CORPORATION

7777 W. BLUEMOUND RD. P.O. BOX 13819 MILWAUKEE, WI 53213

Visit Hal Leonard Online at
www.halleonard.com

FORTY SONGS FOR A BETTER WORLD

Contents

ALL YOU NEED IS LOVE

Words and Music by JOHN LENNON
and PAUL McCARTNEY

CANDLE ON THE WATER

from Walt Disney's PETE'S DRAGON

Words and Music by AL KASHA
and JOEL HIRSCHHORN

I'll be your can-dle on the wa-ter, my love for you will al-ways
I'll be your can-dle on the wa-ter 'til ev-'ry wave is warm and

burn. I know you're lost and drift-ing, but the clouds are lift-ing.
bright. My soul is there be-side you, let this can-dle guide you;

Don't give up; you have some-where to turn.
soon you'll see a gold-en stream of

light.

BLACKBIRD

Words and Music by JOHN LENNON
and PAUL McCARTNEY

Slowly and smoothly

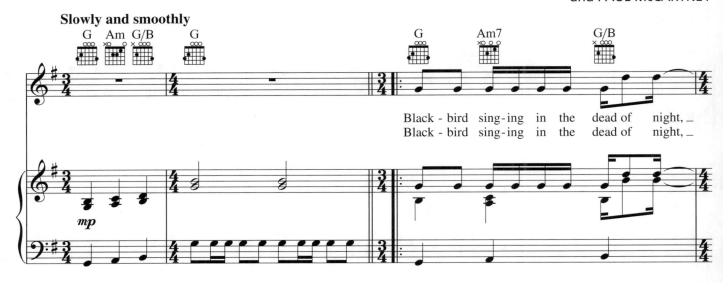

Black - bird sing-ing in the dead of night, ___
Black - bird sing-ing in the dead of night, ___

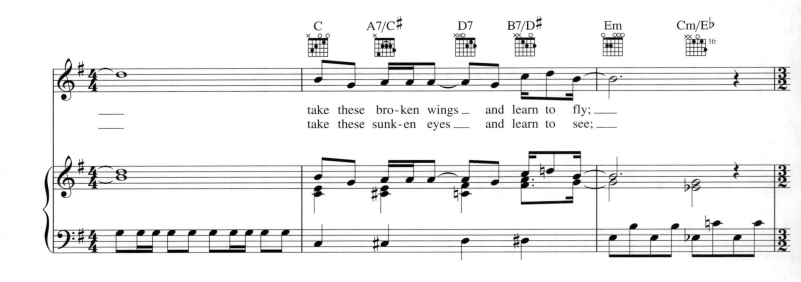

take these bro-ken wings ___ and learn to fly; ___
take these sunk-en eyes ___ and learn to see; ___

all your life ___ you were on-ly wait-ing for this mo-ment to a -
all your life ___ you were on-ly wait-ing for this mo-ment to be

BLESS THE BEASTS AND CHILDREN

from BLESS THE BEASTS AND CHILDREN

Words and Music by BARRY DeVORZON
and PERRY BOTKIN, JR.

Warmly

mp

With pedal

Bless the beasts and the chil - dren,

for in this world _____ they have no voice, _____ they

have no choice. _____ Bless the beasts and the

(Bring out melody)

CHANGE THE WORLD

Words and Music by WAYNE KIRKPATRICK,
GORDON KENNEDY and TOMMY SIMS

CIRCLE OF LIFE
from Walt Disney Pictures' THE LION KING

Music by ELTON JOHN
Lyrics by TIM RICE

From the

CLIMB EV'RY MOUNTAIN
from THE SOUND OF MUSIC

Lyrics by OSCAR HAMMERSTEIN II
Music by RICHARD RODGERS

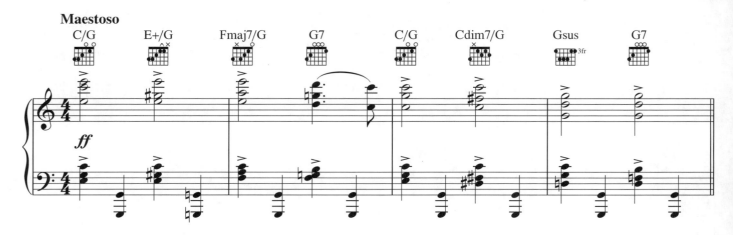

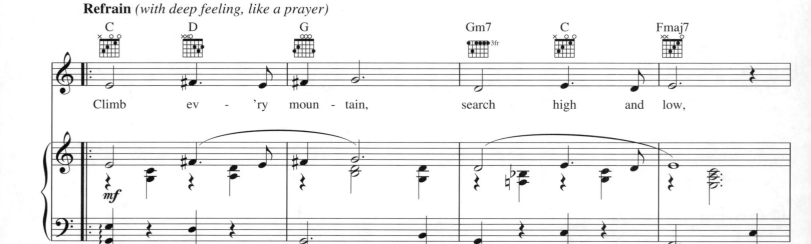

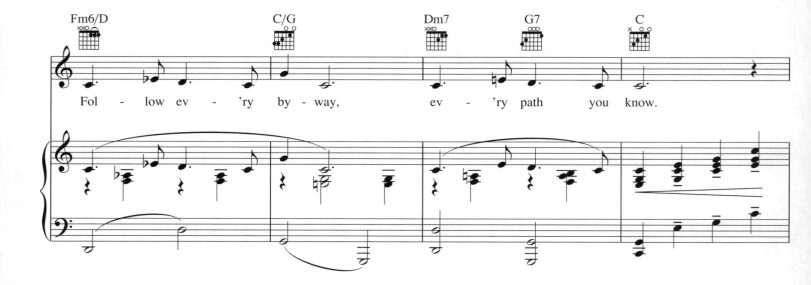

COLORS OF THE WIND

from Walt Disney's POCAHONTAS

Music by ALAN MENKEN
Lyrics by STEPHEN SCHWARTZ

COUNT YOUR BLESSINGS INSTEAD OF SHEEP

from the Motion Picture Irving Berlin's WHITE CHRISTMAS

Words and Music by
IRVING BERLIN

EBONY AND IVORY

Words and Music by
PAUL McCARTNEY

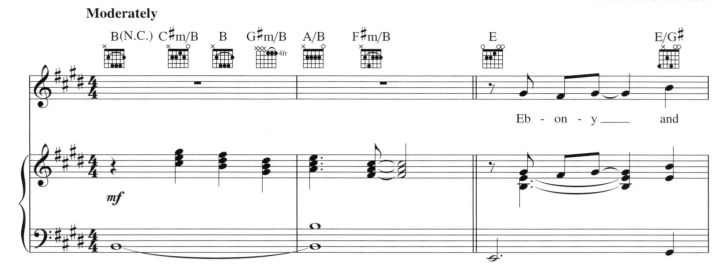

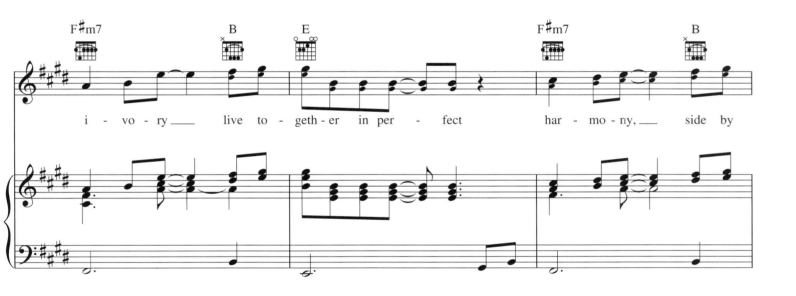

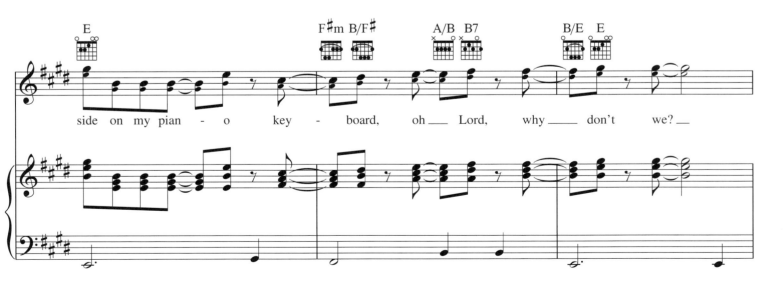

i - vo - ry ___ live to - geth - er in per - fect har - mo - ny, ___ side by

side on my pian - o key - board, oh ___ Lord, why ___ don't we? ___

Eb - on - y, ___

EVERYTHING IS BEAUTIFUL

Words and Music by
RAY STEVENS

heav - en the world's gon - na find _____ a way. _____

1. There is none so blind _____ as he who will not
2. *(See additional lyrics)*

see. _____ We must not close our minds, _____ we must let our thoughts be

free. _____ For ev - 'ry hour that pass - es by _____

Additional Lyrics

2. We shouldn't care about the length of his hair or the color of his skin,
Don't worry about what shows from without but the love that lies within,
We gonna get it all together now and everything gonna work out fine,
Just take a little time to look on the good side, my friend, and straighten it out in your mind.

FRIENDS

Words and Music by MICHAEL W. SMITH
and DEBORAH D. SMITH

FROM A DISTANCE

Words and Music by
JULIE GOLD

GIVE PEACE A CHANCE

Words and Music by
JOHN LENNON

GOD BLESS THE U.S.A.

Words and Music by
LEE GREENWOOD

If to-mor-row all the things were gone I'd worked for all my life and I had to start a-gain with just my chil-dren and my wife, I'd thank my luck-y stars to be

IF I RULED THE WORLD

from PICKWICK

Words by LESLIE BRICUSSE
Music by CYRIL ORNADEL

Steady, moderate tempo

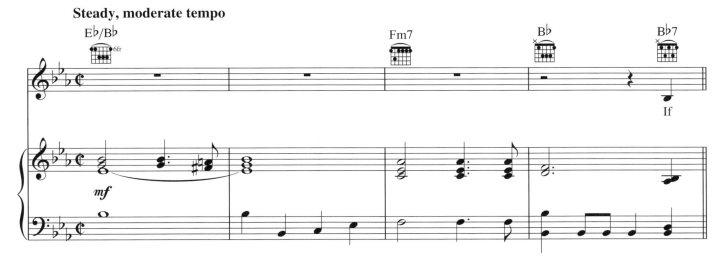

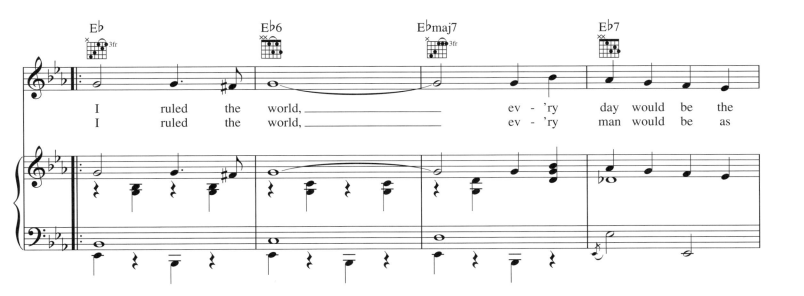

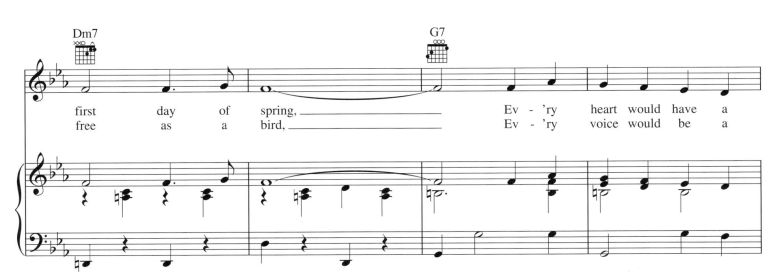

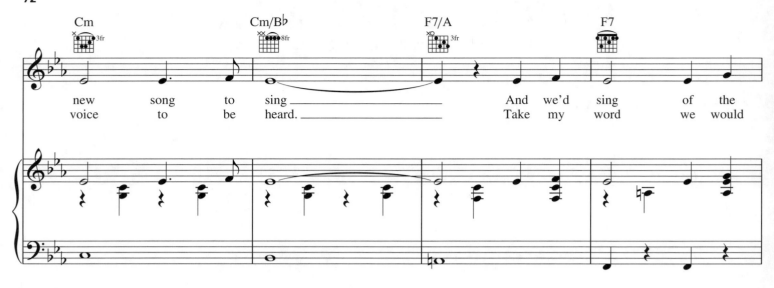

new song to sing _____ And we'd sing of the
voice to be heard. _____ Take my word we would

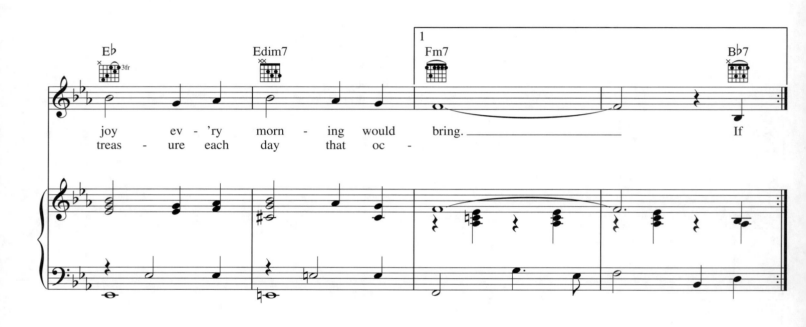

joy ev - 'ry morn - ing would bring. _____ If
treas - ure each day that oc -

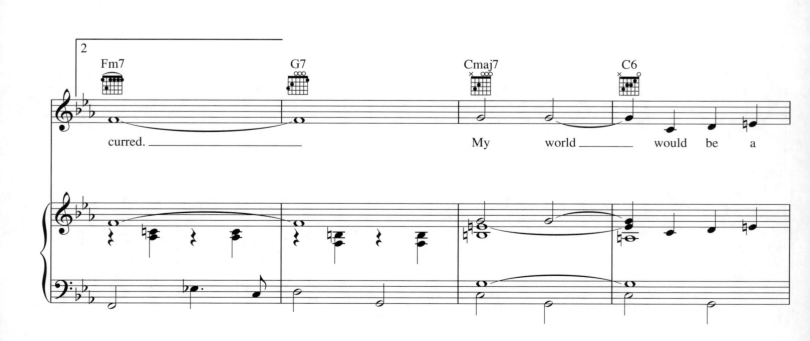

curred. _____ My world _____ would be a

GONNA BUILD A MOUNTAIN

from the Musical Production STOP THE WORLD–I WANT TO GET OFF

Words and Music by LESLIE BRICUSSE
and ANTHONY NEWLEY

Extra Verses

Gonna build a heaven from a little hell.
Gonna build a heaven, and I know darn well,
With a fine young son to take my place
There'll be a sun in my heaven on earth
With the good Lord's grace.

Gonna build a mountain from a little hill.
Gonna build a mountain – least I hope I will.
Gonna build a mountain – gonna build it high.
I don't know how I'm gonna do it –
Only know I'm gonna try.

HE AIN'T HEAVY...
HE'S MY BROTHER

Words and Music by BOB RUSSELL
and BOBBY SCOTT

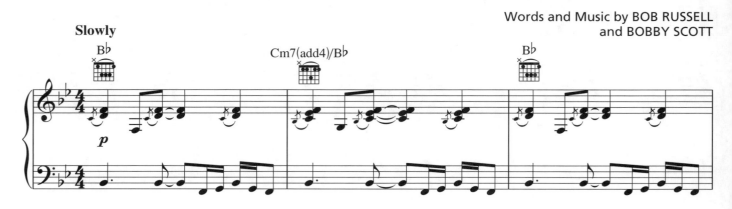

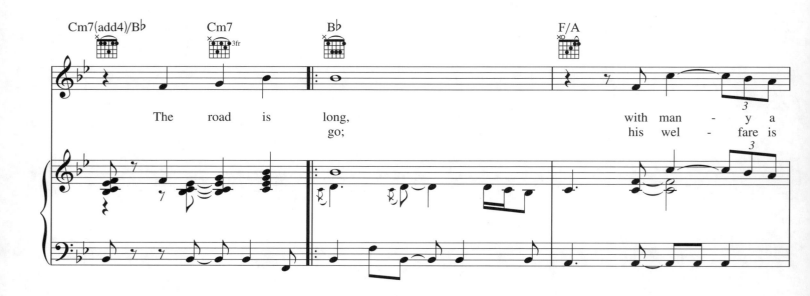

The road is long,
go;
with man - y a
his wel - fare is

wind - ing turn _____ that leads _ us to who knows
my con - cern. _____ No bur - den is he to

IF I HAD A HAMMER

(The Hammer Song)

Words and Music by LEE HAYS
and PETE SEEGER

IF WE ONLY HAVE LOVE
(Quand On N'a Que L'amour)
from JACQUES BREL IS ALIVE AND WELL AND LIVING IN PARIS

Original French Lyrics by JACQUES BREL
Music by JACQUES BREL
English Lyrics by MORT SHUMAN and ERIC BLAU

for the song that we sing,
and we'll drink from the Grail,
then we'll have a way out.
to be born once a - gain.

Then with noth - ing at all,
but the lit - tle we are,

we'll have con-quered all time,
all space,
the sun,
and the
stars.

rit.

IMAGINE

Words and Music by
JOHN LENNON

THE IMPOSSIBLE DREAM
(The Quest)
from MAN OF LA MANCHA

Lyric by JOE DARION
Music by MITCH LEIGH

Tempo di Bolero

JUST ONE DREAM

from GOLDEN DREAMS at Disney's California Adventure Park

Lyrics by JOHN BETTIS
Music by WALTER AFANASIEFF

an - y - thing _ we start. _ An - y - thing _____ can be done _____ with just one _

dream. One friend; _ you know, that's all _ it takes _

_____ is just _ one friend _ to lend _ a hand; _ a help - ing hand, _ that's all _ it takes. _

One smile; _ some - times that's all _ it takes _

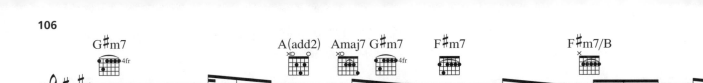

an - y - thing __ we start. __ An - y - thing can be done _____ with just one __

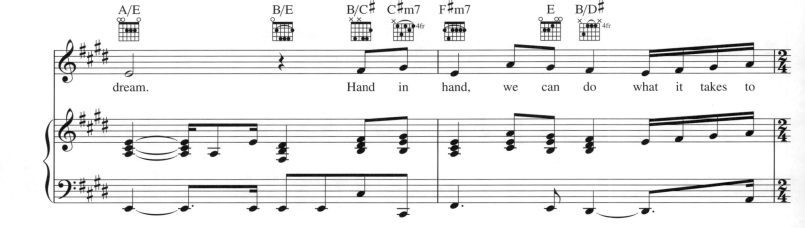

dream. Hand in hand, we can do what it takes to

make our dreams __ come true; _____ each __ of

Freely

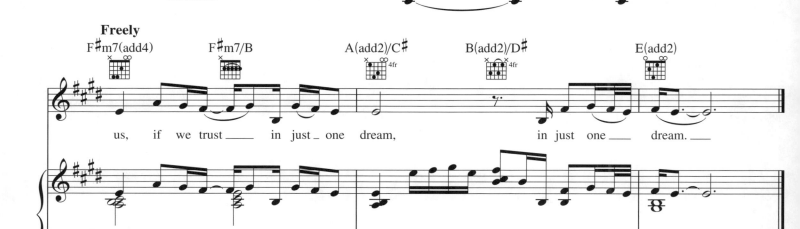

us, if we trust _____ in just __ one dream, in just one _____ dream. __

LET'S GET TOGETHER

Words and Music by
CHET POWERS

Love is but the
Some will come and
If you heard the

song we sing, and fear's the way we die. _____
some will go, and we shall sure - ly pass. _____
song I sing, we you must un - der - stand. _____

You can make the moun-tains ring, ___ or
When the one who left us here, ___ re -
You hold the ___ key to love ___ and

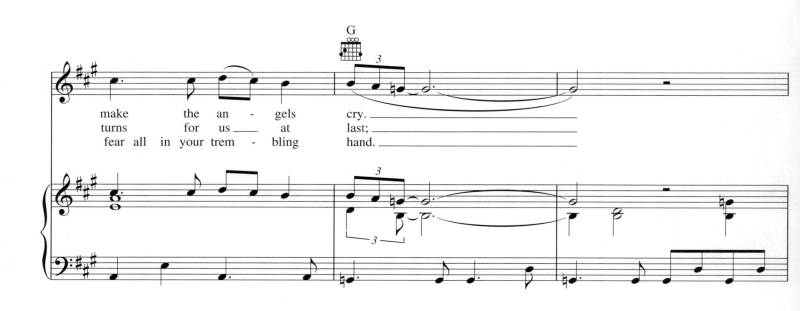

make the an - gels cry. _____
turns for us ___ at last; _____
fear all in your trem - bling hand. _____

Know the dove is on the wing, _ and you need not ___ know
we are but a mo - ment's sun - light, fad - ing on the
One key un - locks them both you know and it's at your ___ com -

LOST IN THE STARS
from the Musical Production LOST IN THE STARS

Words by MAXWELL ANDERSON
Music by KURT WEILL

PUT ON A HAPPY FACE

from BYE BYE BIRDIE

Lyric by LEE ADAMS
Music by CHARLES STROUSE

THE RAINBOW CONNECTION
from THE MUPPET MOVIE

Words and Music by PAUL WILLIAMS
and KENNETH L. ASCHER

Moderately, with a lilt

Why are there so man-y songs a-bout rain-bows, and
Who said that ev-'ry wish would be heard and an-swered when

what's on the oth-er side? ____
wished on the morn-ing star? ____

Rain-bows are vi-sions, ____ but on-ly il-lu-sions, and
Some-bod-y thought of that, and some-one be-lieved it;

REACH OUT AND TOUCH
(Somebody's Hand)

Words and Music by NICKOLAS ASHFORD
and VALERIE SIMPSON

TEARS IN HEAVEN

Words and Music by ERIC CLAPTON
and WILL JENNINGS

Be-yond   the   door ____   there's peace, I'm sure, __

and I know ___ there'll be no more ___ tears in heav-

en.

WHAT THE WORLD NEEDS NOW IS LOVE

Lyric by HAL DAVID
Music by BURT BACHARACH

What the

world needs now is love, sweet love.

It's the on-ly thing _____ that there's just _____ too lit-tle of. What the

TOMORROW
from the Musical Production ANNIE

Lyric by MARTIN CHARNIN
Music by CHARLES STROUSE

Moderately slow

The sun-'ll come out _____ to-mor-row,

bet your bot-tom dol-lar that to-mor-row _____ there'll be

sun! Jus' think-ing a-bout _____ to-mor-row

TURN! TURN! TURN!
(To Everything There Is a Season)

Words from the Book of Ecclesiastes
Adaptation and Music by PETE SEEGER

Moderately slow, in 2

WE ARE FAMILY

Words and Music by NILE RODGERS
and BERNARD EDWARDS

(Yeah, yeah, yeah, ___ yeah, yeah, yeah.) ___

Ev - 'ry - one ___ can see ___ we're to - geth -

you do, you won't go wrong, — oh no. This is our fam - 'ly jewel, yeah, — yeah. —

D.S. al Coda

CODA

— Get up, ev - 'ry - bod - y. —

— Jump! Here we go.

WE ARE THE WORLD

Words and Music by LIONEL RICHIE
and MICHAEL JACKSON

WHAT A WONDERFUL WORLD

Words and Music by GEORGE DAVID WEISS
and BOB THIELE

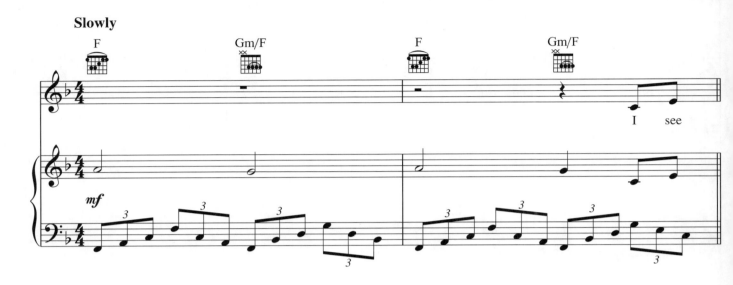

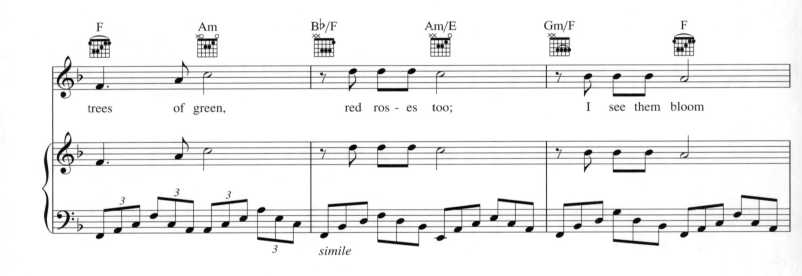

WITH A LITTLE HELP FROM MY FRIENDS

Words and Music by JOHN LENNON
and PAUL McCARTNEY

YOU RAISE ME UP

Words and Music by BRENDAN GRAHAM
and ROLF LOVLAND

Moderately slow

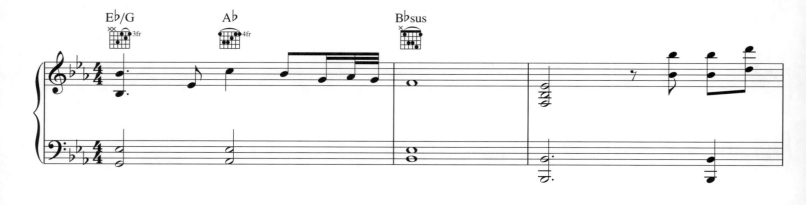

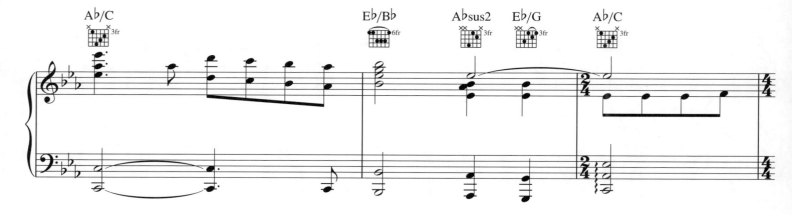

YOU'VE GOT A FRIEND

Words and Music by
CAROLE KING

*Vocal harmony sung 2nd time only.

YOU'VE GOT A FRIEND IN ME

from Walt Disney's TOY STORY

Music and Lyrics by
RANDY NEWMAN

YOU'LL NEVER WALK ALONE
from CAROUSEL

Music by RICHARD RODGERS
Lyrics by OSCAR HAMMERSTEIN II

Andantino molto cantabile

(with great warmth, like a hymn)

* alternate lyric: hold your head up high

blown _____ Walk on, walk on, with

hope in your heart, And you'll nev - er walk a -

lone, _____ You'll nev - er walk a -

lone! _____ When you lone! _____

MORE INSPIRATIONAL
SONGBOOKS FROM HAL LEONARD

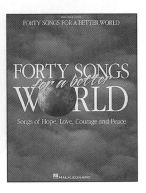

GOD BLESS AMERICA®

FOR THE BENEFIT OF THE TWIN TOWERS FUND

This special matching folio features 15 inspiring patriotic songs performed by top artists. Includes: Amazing Grace (Tramaine Hawkins) ★ America the Beautiful (Frank Sinatra) ★ Blowin' in the Wind (Bob Dylan) ★ Bridge over Troubled Water (Simon & Garfunkel) ★ Coming Out of the Dark (Gloria Estefan) ★ God Bless America® (Celine Dion) ★ God Bless the U.S.A. (Lee Greenwood) ★ Hero (Mariah Carey) ★ Land of Hope and Dreams (Bruce Springsteen and the E Street Band) ★ Lean on Me (Bill Withers) ★ Peaceful World (John Mellencamp) ★ The Star Spangled Banner (The Mormon Tabernacle Choir) ★ There's a Hero (Billy Gilman) ★ This Land Is Your Land (Peter Seeger) ★ We Shall Overcome (Mahalia Jackson).

_____00313196 Piano/Vocal/Guitar $16.95

IRVING BERLIN'S
GOD BLESS AMERICA® & OTHER SONGS FOR A BETTER NATION

This songbook features 35 songs to unite all Americans: Abraham, Martin and John ★ Amazing Grace ★ America ★ America the Beautiful ★ Battle Hymn of the Republic ★ Everything Is Beautiful ★ From a Distance ★ God Bless America® ★ God of Our Fathers ★ He Ain't Heavy...He's My Brother ★ I Believe ★ If I Had a Hammer ★ Imagine ★ Last Night I Had the Strangest Dream ★ Let Freedom Ring ★ Let There Be Peace on Earth ★ The Lord's Prayer ★ My Country 'Tis of Thee (America) ★ Pray for Our Nation ★ Precious Lord, Take My Hand ★ The Star Spangled Banner ★ Stars and Stripes Forever ★ This Is a Great Country ★ This Is My Country ★ This Land Is Your Land ★ United We Stand ★ We Shall Overcome ★ What a Wonderful World ★ What the World Needs Now Is Love ★ You'll Never Walk Alone ★ You're a Grand Old Flag ★ and more.

_____00310825 Piano/Vocal/Guitar $12.95

FORTY SONGS FOR A BETTER WORLD

40 songs with a message, including: All You Need Is Love ★ Blackbird ★ Bless the Beasts and Children ★ Candle on the Water ★ Child of Mine ★ Circle of Life ★ Colors of the Wind ★ Count Your Blessings Instead of Sheep ★ Ebony and Ivory ★ Everything Is Beautiful ★ The Flower That Shattered the Stone ★ Friends ★ From a Distance ★ God Bless the U.S.A. ★ Gonna Build a Mountain ★ He Ain't Heavy...He's My Brother ★ I Am Your Child ★ I Believe ★ If I Had a Hammer (The Hammer Song) ★ If I Ruled the World ★ If We Only Have Love (Quand on N'a Que L'amour) ★ Imagine ★ The Impossible Dream (The Quest) ★ In Harmony ★ Let's Get Together ★ Lost in the Stars ★ Love Can Build a Bridge ★ Love in Any Language ★ Make Your Own Kind of Music ★ One Song ★ Ordinary Miracles ★ The Rainbow Connection ★ Tears in Heaven ★ Turn! Turn! Turn! (To Everything There Is a Season) ★ What a Wonderful World ★ What the World Needs Now Is Love ★ With a Little Help from My Friends ★ You'll Never Walk Alone ★ You've Got a Friend ★ You've Got to Be Carefully Taught.

_____00310096 Piano/Vocal/Guitar $15.95

LET FREEDOM RING!

The Phillip Keveren Series

15 favorites celebrating the land of the free, including: America, the Beautiful ★ Anchors Aweigh ★ Battle Hymn of the Republic ★ Eternal Father, Strong to Save ★ God Bless Our Native Land ★ God of Our Fathers ★ My Country, 'Tis of Thee (America) ★ Semper Fidelis ★ The Star Spangled Banner ★ Stars and Stripes Forever ★ Washington Post March ★ Yankee Doodle ★ Yankee Doodle Boy ★ You're a Grand Old Flag.

_____00310839 Piano Solo..........................$9.95

FOR MORE INFORMATION, SEE YOUR LOCAL MUSIC DEALER, OR WRITE TO:

HAL•LEONARD®
CORPORATION
7777 W. BLUEMOUND RD. P.O. BOX 13819 MILWAUKEE, WI 53213

Visit Hal Leonard Online at
www.halleonard.com

Prices, contents and availability subject to change without notice.

The Finest Inspirational Music

Songbooks arranged for piano, voice, and guitar.

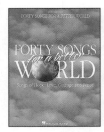

40 SONGS FOR A BETTER WORLD

40 songs with a message, including: All You Need Is Love • Bless the Beasts and Children • Colors of the Wind • Everything Is Beautiful • He Ain't Heavy...He's My Brother • I Am Your Child • Love Can Build a Bridge • What a Wonderful World • What the World Needs Now Is Love • You've Got a Friend • more.
00310096.............................$15.95

THE BEST PRAISE & WORSHIP SONGS EVER

80 all-time favorites: Awesome God • Breathe • Days of Elijah • Here I Am to Worship • I Could Sing of Your Love Forever • Open the Eyes of My Heart • Shout to the Lord • We Bow Down • dozens more.
00311057.....................$19.95

THE BIG BOOK OF CONTEMPORARY CHRISTIAN FAVORITES

50 of today's top CCM hits: Always Have, Always Will • Angels • El Shaddai • Find a Way • Friends • The Great Divide • I Will Be Here • I'll Lead You Home • Jesus Freak • Let Us Pray • Love in Any Language • A Maze of Grace • People Need the Lord • Pray • Shine on Us • Speechless • This Love • Thy Word • To Know You • Undivided • Via Dolorosa • Whatever You Ask • Where There Is Faith • Wisdom • and more.
00310021.............................$19.95

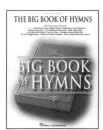

THE BIG BOOK OF HYMNS

An invaluable collection of 125 favorite hymns, including: All Hail the Power of Jesus' Name • Battle Hymn of the Republic • Blessed Assurance • For the Beauty of the Earth • Holy, Holy, Holy • It Is Well with My Soul • Just as I Am • A Mighty Fortress Is Our God • The Old Rugged Cross • Onward Christian Soldiers • Rock of Ages • Sweet By and By • What a Friend We Have in Jesus • Wondrous Love • and more.
00310510.............................$17.95

CHRISTIAN CHILDREN'S SONGBOOK

101 songs from Sunday School, including: Awesome God • The B-I-B-L-E • The Bible Tells Me So • Clap Your Hands • Day by Day • He's Got the Whole World in His Hands • I Am a C-H-R-I-S-T-I-A-N • I'm in the Lord's Army • If You're Happy (And You Know It) • Jesus Loves Me • Kum Ba Yah • Let There Be Peace on Earth • This Little Light of Mine • When the Saints Go Marching In • and more.
00310472.............................$19.95

COUNTRY/GOSPEL U.S.A.

50 songs written for piano/guitar/four-part vocal. Highlights: An American Trilogy • Daddy Sang Bass • He Set Me Free • I Saw the Light • I'll Meet You in the Morning • Kum Ba Yah • Mansion Over the Hilltop • Love Lifted Me • Turn Your Radio On • When the Saints Go Marching In • many more.
00240139.............................$10.95

FAVORITE HYMNS

71 all-time favorites, including: Amazing Grace • Ave Maria • Christ the Lord Is Risen Today • Crown Him with Many Crowns • Faith of Our Fathers • He's Got the Whole World in His Hands • In the Sweet By and By • Jesus Loves Me! • Just a Closer Walk With Thee • Kum Ba Yah • A Mighty Fortress Is Our God • Onward Christian Soldiers • Rock of Ages • Swing Low, Sweet Chariot • Were You There? • and many more.
00490436 ....$12.95

HE IS EXALTED

MUSIC FOR BLENDED WORSHIP
52 beloved hymns and choruses: Awesome God • How Great Thou Art • Lord, I Lift Your Name on High • O Worship the King • Shout to the Lord • The Wonderful Cross • more!
00311068.....................$14.95

I COULD SING OF YOUR LOVE FOREVER

Some of today's most popular CCM artists and their songs are included in this matching folio. Songs: Did You Feel the Mountains Tremble? (Matt Redman) • The Happy Song (Delirious?) • I Could Sing of Your Love Forever (Sonicflood) • Open the Eyes of My Heart (Praise Band) • Pour Out Your Spirit (Tom Lane) • Trading My Sorrows (Darrell Evans) • You Are Merciful to Me (Ian White) • and more.
00306380.............................$14.95

OUR GOD REIGNS

A collection of over 70 songs of praise and worship, including: El Shaddai • Find Us Faithful • His Eyes • Holy Ground • How Majestic Is Your Name • Proclaim the Glory of the Lord • Sing Your Praise to the Lord • Thy Word • and more.
00311695.....................$17.95

SONGS FROM PASSION

This great collection features 14 songs from the recordings *Better Is One Day* and *Live Worship from the 268 Generation*. Includes: Be Glorified • Every Move I Make • Freedom Song • The Heart of Worship • I Will Exalt Your Name • I've Found Jesus • We Fall Down • You Alone • You Are My King • more.
00306345.............................$12.95

TOP CHRISTIAN HITS OF 2003-2004

Your favorites by Avalon, Audio Adrenaline, MercyMe, Stacie Orrico, Third Day and many others! Includes: All About Love • Different Kind of Free • Everything to Me • God of All • Holy • I Can Only Imagine • I Still Believe • I Thank You • It Is You • Legacy • Meant to Live • Pray • Say It Loud • Show Me Your Glory • more.
00311102.............................$14.95

TRADITIONAL GOSPEL

21 songs, including: His Eye Is On The Sparrow • How Great Thou Art • Just a Closer Walk with Thee • The Old Rugged Cross • Peace in the Valley • Take My Hand, Precious Lord.
00361361.....................$8.95

ULTIMATE GOSPEL – 100 SONGS OF DEVOTION

An impressive collection of 100 Gospel favorites, including: El Shaddai • His Eye Is on the Sparrow • How Great Thou Art • Just a Closer Walk with Thee • Lead Me, Guide Me • (There'll Be) Peace in the Valley (For Me) • Precious Lord, Take My Hand • Wings of a Dove • more.
00241009.............................$19.95